The Ministry
of Ushers

Gregory F. Smith, O. Carm.

THE LITURGICAL PRESS

COLLEGEVILLE, MINNESOTA 56321

CONTENTS

It was on a New Year's Eve some years back that I first came to an awareness of the important contribution an usher can make to a worship experience. I had accepted the published invitation of another Christian community to join them for a prayer service on the occasion. Prepared to be somewhat ill at ease, I entered the church only to discover that I need have had no misgivings. A member of the community obviously charged with the task made me warmly welcome. Having introduced herself, she showed me to the cloakroom, where I was invited to hang my coat and deposit my overshoes, if I so wished. Learning that I was a total stranger, she introduced me to several members of the gathering, and after supplying a program for the evening, she led me to the front of the worship area where others had already gathered. I did not meet her again, yet the pleasant demeanor and open cordiality of that usher set the whole tone of a beautifully memorable evening. From the moment I entered the church I was made to feel at home by someone who seemed sincerely glad that I had come. I must confess, however, that I came away with an admiration not untinged with envy for a Christian community blessed with ushers so capable of providing in a brief encounter an experience of genuine Christian hospitality.

5

Our deepening awareness of the need to create and maintain a climate of hospitality within our Eucharistic assemblies has certainly given a new importance to the task of ushers. Ushers have been around for a long time. In many parishes the corps of ushers includes some of the most faithful servants of the parish family. The two basic services they render to the congregation have remained constant and little touched by the liturgical changes of the '70's: they show people to their seats and they take up the collection. While other ministerial groups in parishes are publicly initiated, trained for their special services, and updated through liturgical instruction, ushers are most often allowed to languish as stepchildren of the community: their morale very low, their self-image tarnished, and their ministry little esteemed.

Ushers deserve better. No celebrating community can any longer afford to leave them outside its pastoral concern. In those too rare parishes where the traditional service of ushers has been upgraded to the status of genuine liturgical ministry, where ushers have developed their skills by training and have come to a sense of pride in striving for high standards of excellence in their ministry, their service has become a real blessing to the people and a boost to the quality of worship.

That such advantages may be multiplied is the basic purpose of this pamphlet. It aims to raise the consciousness of pastors and congregations and of ushers themselves so that all will realize the high importance of their role and lift their service to its rightful plane of true ministry. While each parish is different and there must be unique solutions to ushering problems on the local scene, there are common problems and universal needs to be addressed and certain broad principles that should undergird any decisions affecting ushers' ministry. By exploring these for the benefit of all concerned, we hope to make some contribution to the quality of worship in our parishes.

Ushers in history. The ushers of today have descended from a long line of people of God who have gone before them. Their ministry is deeply rooted in Scripture and tradition. The author of the Book of Chronicles, a book coming to us from the third century before Christ, pays particular attention to the part played by the "religious orders" of his time, not only the priests and levites but the lesser orders of cantor and *doorkeeper*. These last, who may have numbered in the hundreds, loomed large in Jerusalem's population at the time and are the progenitors of our ushers today. They comprised the guild of gatekeepers, who had as their assigned task "the guarding of the threshold of the tent, just as their fathers had guarded the entrance of the encampment of the Lord" (1 Chr 9:19).

In order to give this ministry greater importance, the author projects their ritual task in the temple back into the age of David, who died six centuries earlier. It was evidently very early in their history that these "ushers" were assigned the task of receiving the offerings of the faithful. King Josiah (640–609 B.C.), bent on repairing the temple, ordered the high priest Hilkiah to "melt down the precious metals that had been donated to the temple of the Lord, which the doorkeepers had collected from the people" (2 Kgs 22:4). Both Chronicles (9:33) and Jeremiah (35:4) testify that the gatekeepers had rooms in the temple where they stayed when not on duty, since "day and night they had to be ready for service."

In the New Testament we find that the doorkeepers of more ancient times had developed into a paramilitary corps of police at the service of the temple priesthood. On the occasion of the Feast of Booths, when tension ran high among the people who were divided in their attitude toward Jesus, this temple guard was sent to arrest him. More perceptive than their masters, these were won over to Jesus and returned to their masters empty-handed because, they said, "No man ever spoke like that before" (John 7:46). At the end, however, it was the same temple guards that led the crowd to seize Jesus in the Garden of Olives (John 18:3) and who were found guarding the tomb when he rose from the dead (Matt 27:65). St. Luke reveals that it was the captain of the temple guard who arrested Peter and John when they were teaching in the temple (Acts 4:3) and later jailed a whole group of the apostles for the same offense (Acts 5:17–18).

While undoubtedly part of the history of ushering, these temple guards scarcely provide an apt model for contemporary ushers. One thing an usher is not is some sort of latter-day ecclesiastical policeman charged with the exercise of repressive authority. Like everything else he made new, Jesus changed this. Everyone remembers how quick he was to correct his disciples when, acting too officiously, they "began to scold" the women who were bringing their children to him (Matt 19:13).

Among the disciples, ushers can find Gospel models in two of the most lovable, Philip and Andrew. It was the enthusiastic Andrew who brought his brother Simon to Jesus (John 1:42). It was the easily approachable Philip whom the Greeks singled out when they wanted to see Jesus and who with Andrew brought them to the Lord. But it is in John the Baptist that ushers can find the chief exemplar of their role. Like him they are heralds of the Christ of God, drawing attention not to themselves but to him. Ushers are signs pointing to the Way. They are "doors" offering ready access to the living Temple of God, an open invitation to encounter with the Lord.

The more immediate ancestors of ushers are to be found in the clerical order of porter (*ostiarius*, or doorkeeper), instituted in the third century A.D. In those early centuries it was the duty of porters or ushers to guard the door of the church against any intruders who might disturb the service. They also shared with their modern counterparts responsibility for the maintenance of religious decorum during divine worship. By the time the porters' duties came to be stated in the rite of their ordination, they were specified as: "to ring the bells, to open the church and the sacristy, and to open the book for the preacher."

In 1972 Pope Paul VI formally abolished the order of porter. The important task of ushering has been given over to the laity. They may not ring bells, but they must become in their persons a joyous invitation to worship. Even without keys they are charged with becoming an "open door" to holy fellowship. Though the preacher may have no book to be opened, the usher should still be a forerunner of the Word.

A ministry to people. Even before the order of porter was eliminated, the General Instruction of the Roman Missal had acknowledged the special ministry of lay ushers at Holy Mass (68b-c) and had opened this ministry to women (70). The key word here is *ministry*. This is not just a bit of jargon but perhaps the most significant "new" word given to us by the Second Vatican Council. Aware that she makes Christ present, who "did not come to be ministered unto but to minister" (Mark 10:45), the twentieth-century Church sees herself as a "servant Church," with the whole of her membership called to ministry.

Among the servants of God who comprise the membership of the Body of Christ, ushers are called to provide a very special service in their exercise of a true liturgical ministry. They are ministers of the Church and servants of the faith-community in the highest moment of its self-realization when it gathers to celebrate the Eucharist. Every Mass is an action of Christ and the people of God hierarchically assembled. This means that all participants, and particularly those exercising special ministries, must be keenly aware of the ecclesial nature of the celebration.

Because of the nature of their service, ushers especially should bring to their ministry a strong sense of community. They are Church-builders; they shoulder a large measure of the responsibility for helping the local Church realize its identity and thereby become and express its best self through the wor-

9

ship deed that engages it. A prerequisite for those aspiring to quality service in the role of ushers is a commitment to Christ living in his Church, together with a deep sense of being instruments of the community appointed to assist its growth in the Spirit of Jesus. The Church is people gathered in Christ; every usher, therefore, ought to be a "people person."

In many city parishes those who gather for Sunday worship may well be strangers to one another. Some may come to Sunday Mass completely "fed up" with people and desiring nothing more than to sit quietly in a corner somewhere by themselves. Others may labor under the misapprehension that the Eucharist is an opportunity to be alone with God, coming with neither the desire nor a felt need for fellowship. On the other hand, there are always lonely people, young and old alike, who come out of their back rooms thirsting for nothing so much as a warm human contact or a word of cheer.

With a compassion born of his or her own faith, an usher needs to see them all as real people with real human needs. They are not just "paying customers," the midday mob, or the Sunday evening "dregs." Much more precious than the material David gathered for the construction of the temple of Yahweh in Jerusalem, the Sunday assembly, whatever the flaws of its individual parts, is gathered at an infinitely greater cost. They are the living stones used by the Master Builder who is always fashioning a dwelling place for his Spirit. And ushers are not the least of his co-workers.

The Sunday assembly. Our Sunday assemblies should always have about them something of the warm conviviality of a family reunion. A simple gladness in being together should mark each congregation as a community gathered in joyous love to rediscover the bonds of hope and faith that bind the members into a holy fellowship. Each arrival needs to experience the feeling of belonging, a sense that "it is good to be here." A keen perception of mutual acceptance should pervade the gathering so that a feeling of "group" can emerge and a spirit of brotherly and sisterly love can flourish. Hidden fears need to be laid to rest, and individuals need to be encouraged to break out of their private shells and break through that loneliness which is the thing most opposed to God.

True, no Sunday assembly will ever realize perfectly or express adequately the faith-reality of Christian unity in Christ. That would be heaven on earth! Nonetheless, the Lord's Day celebration ought to be a shining moment providing a foretaste and promise of better things to come when, in St. Augustine's beautiful phrase, "We shall be one Christ loving himself," in the great Day of the Lord. Efforts in this direction tend to make Sunday Mass a heavenly experience and to authenticate the Sunday assembly as the great sacrament of unity in Christ. The warm friendliness and open hospitality of ushers provide an essential ingredient that prepares the congregation for the recreative work of the Holy Spirit, who labors mightily in the celebration to make all who share in it "one body, one spirit in Christ."

A ministry to community. Such a faith-vision of the Sunday assembly immediately reveals the great importance of ushers. They, of course, must be the first to share this vision, to make it the motivating force of the service they render to the community, and to accept the challenge it presents to them. If Sunday Mass is ever to become the kind of community experience that can provide a foretaste of heaven, ever so much is demanded of ushers. Perhaps more than all other ministers, they have to be people-oriented. Strangers need to be put at ease; visitors need to be welcomed; the physically and mentally handicapped need to experience the love of the community and to realize their importance to its Christian integrity.

On Sunday it is people who are important. The gathering itself is the most significant element of the worship environment. The

11

ushers' task is to serve the community by helping it to become its best self. This demands of them a charity that is patient and kind with persons who may be difficult, never harsh with those who have their foibles, understanding and compassionate in time of genuine need; a charity that never fails, but is always willing to accept people as they are. Community never just happens. Its development is a labor of love, and none should work at it more earnestly than the ushers.

First things are always important. As servants of the worshiping community, their place at the entrances of the church normally allows ushers the privilege of making the first official contact with those who gather for the Sunday celebration. Before they see the priest or hear the choir, parishioners come face to face with the ushers. This is an enormously important meeting, and, as far as is humanly possible, it ought to be an encounter enlivened by faith. It may well be a lively, even jovial meeting with friends and neighbors. But the eye of faith sees deeper. These are fellow citizens of the saints, brothers and sisters in Christ, assembling to hear his word and to respond with praise and thanks to his Father and ours. An usher's warm welcome and gentle courtesy can set the whole tone for anything that might happen within the hearts of those who gather. Ushers are more than doorkeepers; they are "doors" giving open access to the warmth of holy fellowship in the Spirit of Jesus.

More than other ministers who serve the community as such, ushers have the opportunity to make personal contact with individuals. Even where the celebrant is at one door of the church before or after services, he can greet only a few of those who enter or exit, whereas ushers at all the doors before and after Mass can meet almost everyone. A welcome smile, a word of kindness or reassurance on entering the church, a pleasant greeting or a sincere felicitation given when the parish bulletin is placed in the hands of departing worshipers—these could combine to become the most significant personal contacts the Church makes with people on the occasion of their Sunday worship.

Obviously this significant dimension of the ushers' ministry will fail to accomplish its purpose if it is allowed to become a dull routine. No service to people should ever become perfunctory or merely casual. This is not just a matter of a job to be done and doing it well. Ushering is a sacred ministry, and every usher has to stand ready to bring to bear upon its exercise every personal endowment and all that God has given by way of nature or of grace.

A ministry of grace. A profound interdependence exists among the ministries of all engaged in Sunday worship. Each needs all the others. As the ushers depend on other ministries and profit from their services, they themselves make an important contribution to the efficacy of their fellow ministers. Priests and deacons, ministers of the Word, of the Eucharist, and of music all need the service the usher renders. With all who participate, the ushers are part of the sacrament and forerunners of the Gospel. Being warmly welcomed at the door by the usher is already a Eucharistic grace for the worshipers. It is given to ushers to prepare the soil for the seed of God's Word and to whet appetites for Eucharistic fellowship. The graces mediated by ministers in the sanctuary, the choir, or the pews should find more receptive hearts by reason of other graces mediated by the ushers.

Practical Suggestions

1. Be there. Remember that God's people need you and are depending on you.
2. Arrive early, at least 15 to 20 minutes before the time of the service. Give a moment to silent prayerful preparation for your ministry. Arrange all those things that

need to be readied and then be on hand to greet the people as they arrive.

3. Be at your best. Look pleasant. Check your attire.
4. Take places at *all* the entrances.
5. Make your first word a word of welcome. Keep on the lookout for new members of the parish, for visitors, strangers, or the aged. These last may need special attention.
6. When you recognize newcomers, invite them to meet some of those present. Introduce them. Help them feel at home.

Ministering to joy. The very nature of the Sunday assembly highlights many qualities desirable in ushers. As high feast of the Lord and wedding banquet of the Lamb of God, Sunday Mass is always a joyful occasion. Evening Masses on Saturday or Sunday and early morning Masses will be different from mid-morning or noonday Masses because the mood of the celebrating community is different. But while the time of day will condition the quality of joy anyone is able to bring to the celebration, the joy can never be eliminated. Ushers are called to minister to this joy, the first fruit of the Spirit of Jesus. The stern visage of the beadle ill becomes an usher's countenance. While the responsibility entrusted to them is serious, ushers should serve with obvious pleasure. As C. S. Lewis says, "Joy is the serious business of heaven." Cold, mechanical, impersonal, and aloof ushering is depressing to churchgoers, whereas the sight of good men and women radiating joy as they serve the community is a heartwarming experience.

Ushers, representing the community, are called upon to function as hosts and hostesses. It is therefore incumbent upon them to bring to their service a sincere cordiality enlivened by a desire that all to whom they minister should really enjoy their participation in the Sunday Eucharist. For that to happen, people need to feel at home, at ease with one another, wanted, welcome. Here the ushers' role is decisive in creating an atmosphere of hospitality and friendliness among the members of the assembly. It is crucial in helping people to shed the inhibitions and rigidity too long associated with "going to church." So the pleasant demeanor and welcome smile of the usher are important.

Such cordiality is a "salty" thing that adds the tang of joy and the flavor of festivity to the Sunday experience. It is an antidote to the weekday drabness that is an inevitable part of the burden so many people bring with them to Mass. It serves to lift Sunday above the plane of the ordinary to where it can more easily be appreciated as the great festival of Christians. The warm smiles, friendly courtesy, and gentle concern that should characterize all ushers' contacts with members of the community—qualities most often silent, unobtrusive, inconspicuous, and therefore unnoticed—are powerful aids toward making Sunday Mass a true festivity.

Dependability. If an usher is appointed to serve at a service, he or she has to be there. This is not merely a matter of "covering" a door or an aisle, though this is far from unimportant. The ushers' dependability is of consequence to parishioners, to whom they become "landmarks." The glimpse of an usher who is always there gives people a sense of familiarity and stability, the feeling of a pleasant homecoming. The usher is a sign of the caring community. The very sight of the ushers communicates a sense of welcome repose. "The ushers are here. All is well. Everything is under control. I can depend on them because they are concerned for me."

Kindness. Traditionally, as we have seen, the preservation of good order within the community has been part of the ushers' ministry. They order processions and the movement of people, and they see to it that the congregation is seated compactly in the worship area. Such ministry can be effective, however, only when it is wholly leavened with kindness. Ushers are not some sort of ecclesiastical policemen or policewomen. They are hosts, not marshals. Any taint of officialism or hint of pomposity has to be rejected by ushers as unworthy of their ministry. Kindness is the rule; understanding is the principle.

People are people; each is unique and all kinds make up the People of God. Each parish presents a cross section of the Church. There are teenagers: sometimes thoughtless, often bored or even rebellious. There are the elderly: querulous perhaps, hard of hearing, halt or lame. Young adults with growing families and infants in arms are there, too. All have special needs to which ushers are called to minister with the unfailing kindness people rightly expect from servants of the Church.

On that occasion which foreshadowed the Eucharist (Mark 6) when the apostles, taking on the role of ushers, succeeded in handling an excited crowd of five thousand hungry people, getting them to sit on the ground in groups of fifty or a hundred "neatly arranged like flower beds," it could not have been an easy task. Certainly every parish since has had its "problem people." There are those who will resist the well-meaning and necessary efforts of ushers to seat the congregation compactly so that it will form a united community without vacant spaces. There are claustrophobiacs who simply must sit near the door or at the end of a pew. Others for no good or apparent reason will insist on standing in the rear of the church when there is ample seating available.

Ushers' deep concern for the community as a whole and for their ministry of facilitating the common task of prayer and action has to be balanced by a keen sensitivity to people's feelings and the personal needs of individuals. This calls for that "gentle graciousness" which St. Paul so highly recommends to the Philippians (4:5). It goes by many names, all of which speak to

16

ushers. It is patience and forbearance, tolerance and magnanimity; it is that "splendor of charity" called kindness.

Accenting the positive. The problems ushers meet are most often human problems. Handling them effectively calls for delicate skill. Even when an usher chooses rightly, that is, adding honey rather than vinegar to speech, success in handling a problem may not be radiant. Nevertheless, much can be accomplished with smiles and warmth, good humor and soft-spoken requests made with the usher's obvious eagerness to help everyone pray better. Courtesy demands that any directive given by an usher should never smack of criticism or convey annoyance. Even in the most trying circumstances, a kind usher will try to make directives positive. For example:

Negative: "Mass has begun. You can't use this door!"
Positive: "In order to avoid disturbing the opening rites, would you be so kind as to use the rear door?"

Negative: "Would you kids shut up!"
Positive: "We need your help. Would you young people help us to promote quiet in our place of worship?"

Negative: "Move on, folks. You're blocking the entrance!"
Positive: "Could you folks please visit over here where the crowd won't interfere with your conversation?"

Reverence. While liturgy is always the work of creatures, it is never earthbound but always invites to the experience of mystery. Under the headship of Jesus, "the first-born of every creature" (Col 1:15), a Spirit-filled people reaches out to give the Father praise and adoration, glory and thanks. The work of the Sunday assembly is filled with an awareness of God; it is wholly God-centered. The demands of hospitality must be met, as we have seen, but the manner of the usher should invite to "worship in spirit and in truth."

Reverence is high on the list of desirable qualities in any

usher. This is really a matter of the ushers' faith and of letting that faith shine through in action and attitude. Faith sees beyond the faces of people, beneath the surface of things. Whatever their characteristics, these people are brothers and sisters dear to us in the family of God; whatever their sinfulness, they are still God's holy people. Only a sense of the holy and an awareness of the "holy thing" that happens when the Church assembles and the Mystical Body of Christ takes on visible, tangible, audible reality can bring to ushers' service that sense of reverence and awe that are essential ingredients of Sunday worship.

This reverent attitude is not to be identified with the whispered greetings of a funeral parlor or the exaggerated solemnity of a mortician; but neither is it consonant with a frivolity that demeans the occasion or a nonchalance that makes it inconsequential. Joy, yes, but joy in the mystery: "Christ among you, your hope of glory" (Col 1:27). By the radiance of their countenances, by the way they stand and move and look, ushers can and should convey to all present the sense that Sunday is a special day and Sunday Mass a very special happening. This means that the ushers' response to the liturgy should be one of depth and authenticity, of reverence for all in the assembly and respect for everything they do and use in carrying out their ministry.

Practical Suggestions

1. If you cannot function for an appointed service, it is your responsibility to provide a substitute.
2. Cultivate a sense of humor in the face of difficulty. Never show irritation. Have a non-judgmental attitude.
3. Be sure that everything you do *or do not do* contributes to the reverent quiet that should prevail during times of prayer and the Liturgy of the Word. It is a thoughtless irreverence toward the Word of God and a disrespect for people to seat latecomers at these times.

18

4. An usher may stop late arrivals from disturbing the praying, listening assembly by standing firmly at the foot of the aisle.
5. Where seating reserved for the purpose is not available for those arriving during the Liturgy of the Word, request quietly that they wait for the earliest opportunity to be seated.
6. Handle unsupervised children gently, tactfully. They are people, too. Yet they cannot be allowed to wander in and out to the disturbance of the assembly. If they must leave, chairs might be provided for them in the foyer until they can return opportunely.
7. Do not forget that you are also part of the community at worship.

Liturgical ministry. As a ministerial group, ushers exercise their functions outside the sanctuary. Unfortunately, in the past this has often come to mean apart from the worshiping community. Carried to extremes (habit and routine lead in this direction!), this latter attitude has at times placed ushers wholly at variance with the central thrust of the Sunday Eucharist in their action and their posture. Ushers, therefore, should see themselves first of all as part of the worshiping community and seek to become its most attentive participants. They are not attendants called in from the outside at strategic moments or stagehands chatting idly in the wings as they wait for the time to change the scenery. They are men and women within the assembly, called to render a special service to the group but also engaged with it in divine worship—singing, listening, praying and reflecting, giving and receiving all with the community. Perhaps it is here in their manifest concern for good worship that ushers make their most effective contribution toward making Sunday Mass a good worship experience for those to whom they minister.

This presumes that in their training ushers have moved beyond any merely superficial understanding of what Catholic worship is all about. Their joy in serving should spring from a profound awareness that the Eucharist in which they are so intimately involved proclaims the death and resurrection of Jesus and, as the memorial of the Lord, makes the paschal mystery present in power, a living hope for God's holy people. Their care for the community should flow from a faith-conviction that the liturgy is the "action of Christ and the people of God hierarchically assembled" and from an understanding of the truth that "Christ always associates the Church with himself in this great work wherein God is glorified and men are sanctified" (Constitution on the Liturgy, no. 7).

Not for ushers is the too common vision of the Mass as "just one thing after another," with little coherence among the parts. They should have come to a practical understanding of the real presence of Jesus the Lord within the worshiping community. This is the overarching principle that makes the Mass one great action celebrated in Word and in Work. The gradual intensification of this real presence provides the unifying dynamic of every Eucharistic celebration. Christ is present, really present, when his people gather and his Mystical Body takes on concrete, visible reality. When, enlivened by his Spirit, they pray and sing together, Jesus is there praying. With the proclamation of his word, "something alive and active" (Heb 4:12), a whole new dimension is given to the presence of the risen Lord to his people. They are brought to their feet with twin shouts of recognition: "Glory to you, Lord!—Praise to you, Lord Jesus Christ!" Then as the Word leads to Work, the real presence of Christ takes on that wholly unique sacramental dimension, wherein the ever-dying, ever-rising Savior becomes the unifying food and drink of a pilgrim people. Thus gathered into one Bread, one Body, this people is then scattered to bring Christ's saving presence to the world of our times.

All of this, of course, is communicated through the liturgy in its own tongue, the language of sign and symbol. Since the ushers are themselves part of the Eucharistic sign, they should at least be familiar with this mode of communication, God's chosen medium for communicating life. For "in the liturgy the sanctification of men is signified by signs perceptible to the senses, and is effected in a way which corresponds to each of these signs" (Constitution on the Liturgy, no. 7). Fuller comprehension of the language of the liturgy is something an usher must always strive for with the necessary help of in-service training. If, as the Constitution on the Liturgy states, "composers and singers must be given a genuine liturgical training" (no. 115), it is no less necessary for ministers of hospitality.

Seating people. Such an understanding of the liturgy has a special bearing on one of the important functions of ushers: seating people. The Sunday assembly is a sacrament, a sign of unity in Christ. It should be experienced as a gathering, not a scattering. So it is absolutely crucial for good worship that people be seated together and not at the ends of all the pews with large gaps between. As far as possible, churches should be filled from the front to the back and not vice versa, leaving a bank of empty pews near the altar.

Experience proves that people become very attached to "their pews," so ushers may not always be successful in getting them to change their seating habits. Nevertheless, it is urgent that they do what they can within the bounds of courtesy and without any browbeating to seat people together in the front of the church. Some parish councils have come to the aid of their ushers by authorizing the use of rope devices to cordon off sections of the church that are not needed for sparsely attended Masses or for all Masses in large churches with small congregations, leaving ample seating in the front and center of the worship area. This practice is highly recommended and of proven worth.

In any church, it is good practice to reserve a number of seats in the rear where latecomers can be seated unobtrusively and without disturbing those seated in front of them. While late arrivals should always be treated kindly, they should not be allowed to distract the praying, listening, reflecting assembly already in place. If they cannot be seated quietly in pews reserved for them in the rear, ushers should ask them to wait until they can be seated at an opportune time. Times for silent prayer are *not* such "breaks"! As custodians of the stillness, all ushers should be aware of moments when it is least likely to be infringed upon in seating latecomers. Three such times recommend themselves as opportune:

a) *If there is time before the entrance song,* after the preparation period.

b) *After the opening prayer,* while all are being seated before the first reading. (Here the lector should be watchful to see that everyone is seated before moving to the lectern.)

c) *After the Gospel,* while all are being seated for the homily. If some stragglers arrive during the homily, they should be asked to wait until the people sit for the preparation of gifts. At other times there should be no movement in the aisles. Movement always attracts attention, and nothing the usher does should ever distract from prayer and the proclamation of the Word of God.

Practical Suggestions

1. Before Mass: Put collection baskets in place. See that the "gift table" is prepared and in place. Have ready at hand and in sufficient quantity any participation materials that have to be distributed.

2. After your word of welcome, let your next word be a quiet suggestion that arrivals sit near the front and together with others.

3. When you lead people up the aisle, walk slowly or you will lose them. Do not merely point to a seat, but lead people there personally.

4. If it is your responsibility, the welcoming period is the best time to enlist those who will carry the gifts to the altar.

5. When it is time for the celebration to begin (this would include any preparation period led by a music minister or cantor), allow last-minute arrivals to take care of themselves, cease all movement and go to your stations.

6. The ushers should have a place. It should be furnished so that they can readily assume the postures of the assembly—sitting, standing, kneeling with the community—throughout the liturgy.

The collection. The Sunday collection is certainly not the chief focus of the ministry of ushering. It is, nonetheless, an important part of it. The acceptance of money gifts on Sunday is a most venerable tradition among Christians, going back to the apostolic Church. It seems that St. Paul took up collections "for the saints" wherever he went (see 1 Cor 16:1-2), this being the one thing Peter, James, and John had insisted on when he met with them in Jerusalem and, as Paul asserts, something he was himself "anxious to do" (Gal 2:10).

The taking up of the collection should not be seen as a sordid necessity for keeping up with the operating expenses of the parish plant. For ushers, it is part of their ministry of hospitality, an honorable task that presents to the faithful assembled a special opportunity to share in the Mass action by making a sacrificial offering to be joined to the offering of Christ. The collection has come to be appreciated as an integral part of the Eucharistic celebration with its own place in the rite, when nothing else is going on.

Practical Suggestions

1. After the Creed, gather in the rear of the church and there participate in the general intercessions.
2. Make sure that there are sufficient baskets (plates) and ushers so that undue delay may be avoided.
3. As people are being seated after the general intercessions, take the baskets and begin the collection immediately. The spirit of hospitality demands that people should not feel they are being rushed, but don't waste time. Never embarrass anyone.
4. While the collection is being gathered, one usher, left free for the purpose, should see that the gift-bearers are ready for the procession. When the collection has been gathered into one basket without ado (no sound of jangling coins, please!), one usher leads the procession to the altar, walking with simple dignity and not too quickly. The basket is presented to the priest, and the usher steps aside for the gift-bearers, returning to his/her place immediately without any genuflection.
5. If the gift table must be removed, do so unobtrusively.

The Eucharistic Prayer and Communion. During the entire Eucharistic Prayer, the ushers normally have nothing in particular to do. At this time they share with the entire community the task of personal involvement in the Eucharistic action. There should be no movement in the church at this time, least of all among the ushers. There is no need for them to be walking about or conversing. If the community kneels during the Eucharistic Prayer, the ushers should kneel; if the community stands, they should stand.

When new procedures are being followed, necessitated perhaps by the more recent practice of sharing the communion cup on the Lord's Day, ushers may be involved in ordering the communion procession. Once effective traffic patterns have been established, however, people usually follow them very easily. The ushers' role at this time is minimal: keep alert for possible snags, for a child who is lost or an elderly person who is confused. People in general know what they are doing and do it well. Good ushers let this happen and do nothing at all.

Practical Suggestions

1. Only a genuine emergency should draw an usher from his/her place during the Eucharistic Prayer.
2. Actual need should be the criterion for the ushers' involvement in the communion procession. If directions have to be given, this should be done with warmth and gentleness as becomes ministers of hospitality, especially at the Lord's table. The imperative gestures or stance of a traffic cop are always out of order. Never touch anyone, unless it is with the helping hand that gives needed assistance.
3. During the communion service, nothing else should occupy the ushers' attention. This is not the time to begin preparations for departure!
4. During the meditation after communion, the ushers should be in their place, engaged in their own reflection. Those who habitually leave at this time must be left to their own devices. The ushers' obvious concern for prayerfulness may be by and large the best antidote for such an unfortunate routine.

Dismissal

1. Remain in your places during the prayer after communion and any announcements.
2. With the beginning of the final hymn or the instrumental postlude, go to the doors. In good weather see that they are propped open to provide easy exit for the assembly.
3. Stand ready to take any books or hymnals from the hands of the ministers as they leave.

4. Be available at each door to place bulletins in the hands of those departing; to provide needed assistance for anyone disabled; and to wish all a pleasant good-bye. Remember, this is your final opportunity to bring pleasure to their Sunday experience.
5. Adjust windows, if necessary, and check the church for articles left behind and for litter in the seats or on the floor. In general, see that all is in good order for the next service.

Emergency procedures. In some areas and frequently in small parishes, ushers are hard to come by. It is probably too much to expect, therefore, that every team of ushers should have someone trained in the techniques of artificial respiration and mouth-to-mouth resuscitation. Nonetheless, such persons might well be sought out and enlisted in the ushers' corps. In most areas today, ushers could take free courses in first aid to the sick and injured. Such courses might well add interest or even enthusiasm to the regular ushers' meeting and, more importantly, increase their skills in offering practical assistance at critical moments.

Procedures in case of physical sickness or even sudden death, fire, power failure, and other emergencies should be known and planned in advance. Ushers should have a base of operation where the telephone numbers of the police department, the fire department, public utilities company, ambulance service, and physicians can be prominently posted. Here, too, emergency equipment can be stored: smelling salts, a stretcher, flashlights, candles and matches, a fire extinguisher, etc. Ushers should also be on the lookout for nurses and physicians as they enter the church, making mental note of where they are seated, so that their assistance can be readily sought in time of need.

Striving for excellence. Acutely aware of past shortcomings, the Church today is striving earnestly to improve the quality of Sunday worship. This is a matter of responding to the mind of Christ and following where his Spirit leads. The Spirit functions through many concrete factors such as acoustics, seating arrangement, ventilation, and so on. But because the Church is people, the Spirit works through them with their attitudes and feelings and postures. Most especially the Spirit works through those who minister to the congregation in the role of preacher, lector, musician, Eucharistic minister, or usher. No one is exempt! In the power of the Spirit, all ministers should strive constantly for higher standards of excellence in their ministry; none should strive more assiduously than those engaged in the ministry of hospitality, the ushers. At stake here is the greater glory of God and the greater holiness of his people.

Suggested Rite for the Installation of Ushers

If he has not done so in the homily, the celebrant may afterwards speak briefly of the meaning and importance of the ministry of ushering. Then he may call the candidates forward in these or similar words:

Celebrant: Will those who desire to serve as ushers in the faith-community of *(name of parish)* kindly step forward.

The candidates come from their seats and stand before the celebrant, who greets each warmly and then says to all:

Celebrant: Are you ready to assume the responsibility of the ushers' ministry?

Candidates: We are.

Celebrant: Do you promise to be faithful to your duties and prompt in your service?

Candidates: By the grace of God we do.

Celebrant: "Love your fellow Christians always. And always remember to show hospitality, for by that means some have entertained angels without knowing it" (Heb 13:1-2)

Let us pray.
Lord, our God and gracious Father,
according to the gifts you have given to each,
all of us are called to serve you in different ways
and to render various services to our brothers and sisters
    in the faith.
Yours is the call, yours are the gifts.
Look kindly on these men (and women)
whom you summon to the ministry of hospitality
    among us.
Fill them with the fire of your love,
let them be the instruments of your kindness,
and crown them with joy in your service.
Let their faith shine out so that the warmth
    of their friendliness

will be a sign of your love for us all.
We ask this through Christ our Lord.

All: Amen.

After the prayer the celebrant may wish to invest each usher with an appropriate sign of his/her new role, e.g., a name tag, a cross or medallion, or some identifying garment such as a blazer. This may be done in silence or with these or similar words:

Celebrant: Receive this sign of the ushers' ministry. May you be blessed in the service you render: In the name of the Father and of the Son and of the Holy Spirit.

All: Amen.

The celebrant congratulates each in turn and may then invite the assembly to show their approval by applause.

A petition for the success of the ushers' ministry may be added to the general intercessions.

AN USHER'S PRAYER

Lord, you make all kinds of people, even people like me. In your love you gather them all into your Church. As you gather your people this day, help me to serve them in a Christlike manner, even as your Son served those who gathered about him. Make me prayerful and patient, helpful and understanding, and may I radiate the joy that faith brings as I serve their needs. Give me your strength to support my fellow ministers. May all who assemble to celebrate our common faith in the risen Savior be glad of heart for being here and for having encountered your Son in one another, in our priest, at the tables of the Book and the Bread, and through the ministry of ushers like me. I ask this in Jesus' name. Amen.

ADDITIONAL AIDS FOR LITURGY MINISTERS—

SPEECH AND ORAL READING TECHNIQUES
FOR MASS LECTORS AND COMMENTATORS
By Benedict E. Hardman. A clear and concise manual for the training of liturgical readers. Treats such topics as fear and stagefright, breath control, projection and intonation, phrasing, pause, oral reading techniques, eye contact, pronunciation, and use of public address microphone. 32 pages, paperback, $.75.

PROCLAIMING THE LORD IN OUR MIDST
A parish lector formation program designed by the Archdiocese of Detroit's Office of Christian Worship. Contains sessions on Church, ministry, Scripture, the Liturgy of the Word, and communications. 85 pages in a loose-leaf binder, $5.00.

SPECIAL MINISTERS OF THE EUCHARIST
A program designed by the Archdiocese of Detroit's Office of Christian Worship. Material for sessions on Church, ministry, liturgy, and Eucharistic documents. 92 pages in a loose-leaf binder, $5.00.

CELEBRATING THE EUCHARIST
This top-quality missalette contains the complete texts for Sundays and major feasts to enable the lector, commentator, and other liturgical ministers to prepare at home and become fully familiar with the complete message of the Mass. Single copy sent to home address for $6.00 per year; includes five issues plus Holy Week missalette. Prices for bulk or parish subscription sent upon request.

THE EUCHARIST: ESSENCE, FORM, CELEBRATION
By Johannes H. Emminghaus. Gives a pastoral and practical explanation of the basic structure of the Mass, the historical changes in the celebration of the Mass, and a detailed commentary on each part of the Mass. Called "the best commentary on the new Roman Missal now available in English." An ideal gift or study tool for an usher's renewed understanding and appreciation of the Mass. 229 pages, paperback, $7.50.

THE LITURGICAL YEAR
By Adrian Nocent, O.S.B. A simple, popular, and pastoral presentation of the liturgical year giving biblical and liturgical reflections on the particular liturgical season, the structure and themes of each season, and suggestions from the past to better celebrate the present. Four volumes include Advent, Christmas, and Epiphany; the Lenten season; the Paschal Triduum, the Easter Season, and the Solemnities of the Lord; and Sundays in Ordinary Time. Each volume, $10; four-volume set, $35.00.

Prices subject to change. *Write for free complete catalog.*

You may order these books directly from

THE LITURGICAL PRESS
Collegeville, Minnesota 56321
612-363-2213